21st Century Junior Library

SETTING AND ACHIEVING POSITIVE GOALS

Read and Reflect: A Social-Emotional Guide

Emily Rose

Published in the United States of America by:

CHERRY LAKE PRESS
2395 South Huron Parkway, Suite 200, Ann Arbor, Michigan 48104
www.cherrylakepress.com

Reading Adviser: Beth Walker Gambro, MS, Ed., Reading Consultant, Yorkville, IL
Photo Credits: © Pixel-Shot/Shutterstock.com, cover, 1; © theshots co/Shutterstock.com, 5; © Luis Molinero/Shutterstock.com, 6; © Roman Samborskyi/Shutterstock.com, 7, 21; © enciktepstudio/Shutterstock.com, 8, 9; © Melpomene/Shutterstock.com, 10; © Lucky Business/Shutterstock.com, 11; © GOLFX/Shutterstock.com, 12; © SeventyFour/Shutterstock.com, 15; © antonio diaz/Shutterstock.com, 16; © Monkey Business Images/Shutterstock.com, 17; © Asia Images Group/Shutterstock.com, 18; © espies/Shutterstock.com, 20 [right]; © krakenimages.com/Shutterstock.com, 20 [left]

Cherry Lake Press is an imprint of Cherry Lake Publishing Group.

Library of Congress Cataloging-in-Publication Data

Names: Rose, Emily (School psychologist), author.
Title: Setting and achieving positive goals / by Emily Rose.
Description: Ann Arbor, Michigan : Cherry Lake Publishing, [2022] | Series: Read and reflect: a social-emotional guide | Includes bibliographical references and index. | Audience: Grades 2-3
Identifiers: LCCN 2021036776 (print) | LCCN 2021036777 (ebook) | ISBN 9781534199088 (hardcover) | ISBN 9781668900222 (paperback) | ISBN 9781668901663 (pdf) | ISBN 9781668905982 (ebook)
Subjects: LCSH: Goal (Psychology)—Juvenile literature. | Motivation (Psychology) in children—Juvenile literature.
Classification: LCC BF505.G6 R67 2022 (print) | LCC BF505.G6 (ebook) | DDC 158.1—dc23
LC record available at https://lccn.loc.gov/2021036776
LC ebook record available at https://lccn.loc.gov/2021036777

Cherry Lake Press would like to acknowledge the work of the Partnership for 21st Century Learning, a Network of Battelle for Kids. Please visit http://www.battelleforkids.org/networks/p21 for more information.

Printed in the United States of America
Corporate Graphics

CHERRY LAKE PRESS

CONTENTS

WHAT IS A GOAL?

A goal is something that you can **strive** for to get what you want. Have you ever thought about what you want to be when you grow up? That is a goal. Maybe your goal is to be a teacher or a scientist.

Goals can also be **accomplishments**. For example, you might have a goal to learn how to make your grandma's macaroni and cheese recipe by yourself. Maybe you have a goal to **audition** for the school

What is the one goal that you really want to achieve?

talent show. Setting goals helps us to try new things and grow.

Some goals take a long time to achieve. Those are long-term goals. Some goals take only a short time to achieve. Those are short-term goals. A long-term goal might be to become a **pilot** when you grow up. A short-term goal may be to get an A+ on your next spelling test.

What is one example of a short-term goal and one example of a long-term goal?

What other steps can you think of that a person might take to achieve the goal of becoming a pilot or getting an A+ on a spelling test?

One thing to remember is that all goals, short-term or long-term, are easier to achieve when you break them into steps. Let's talk about how to break big goals into smaller steps in the next chapter!

Ask Questions!

Ask a friend or family member if they have ever set a goal and what advice they can pass along to you.

HOW TO SET A GOAL BY MAKING STEPS

A step that might help you reach the short-term goal of getting an A+ on your spelling test is practicing writing each spelling word three times every day. Another step might be asking someone to help you study the words and spell them out loud.

A small step to achieve the long-term goal of becoming a pilot could be to do your next book report on the history of airplanes. If you know someone who is a

pilot, you could talk to that person about flying planes. Another small step could be to get good grades in school to help you get accepted into flight school one day.

Make a Guess!

Think about a goal you have right now. What are some smaller steps that can help you to achieve that goal?

Because long-term goals take longer to achieve, they often have more steps. When our goals have steps, it's easier to stay on track and know what to do next, even when a goal seems far in the future.

When we know which steps to take, we can make **progress** toward our goals, no matter how big or small!

Think about a goal you achieved in the past. What steps did you take to get there?

Have you ever set a goal but didn't achieve it? What happened? How did you feel?

WHAT IF I DON'T REACH MY GOAL?

Sometimes we might not reach a goal, even when we try really hard. Maybe you studied your spelling words every night but forgot how to spell some of the words on the day of the test. That's okay! Or maybe you decided that you don't want to be a pilot anymore. Instead, you would like to be a writer. That is okay too! Goals can change.

If you don't achieve a goal that you really wanted, here are some things you can do:

- Think about how long you gave yourself to achieve that goal. Would you have come closer to your goal if you had more time or if you made smaller steps?
- Did you ask for help to reach your goal? If not, can you ask for help next time? What could have helped you to achieve that goal?
- Ask yourself *why* you wanted to achieve that goal in the first place. Did you really *have* to achieve it? Is it okay to get a B+ on your spelling test, even though your goal was to get an A+?

Think!

Let's reflect on the questions above. Think of a goal you really wanted to achieve, but either didn't achieve or haven't achieved quite yet. What can you do to help you achieve that goal? Is this goal really meaningful for you, or do you just feel like you should achieve it?

Think about a time you set a goal and got close to achieving it but didn't make it all the way. What important lessons did you learn along the way?

GET A GOAL ROLE MODEL

Everyone has different goals. Maybe you know someone who auditioned for the school talent show, which is *your* goal too! It's often easier to achieve

Do you have someone you look up to? How might that person's wisdom or positive energy help you achieve your goal?

goals when we have a coach, **mentor**, or **role model** to help. Your role model might be a famous athlete or musician. A mentor could be a teacher or other trusted adult. Someone who has achieved success in your goal area might be willing to coach you toward your goal.

A goal role model can be someone who has achieved the goal you are seeking. They can also be someone who has no **experience** with this goal but who

Who is a person in your life whom you can lean on to help reach your goal?

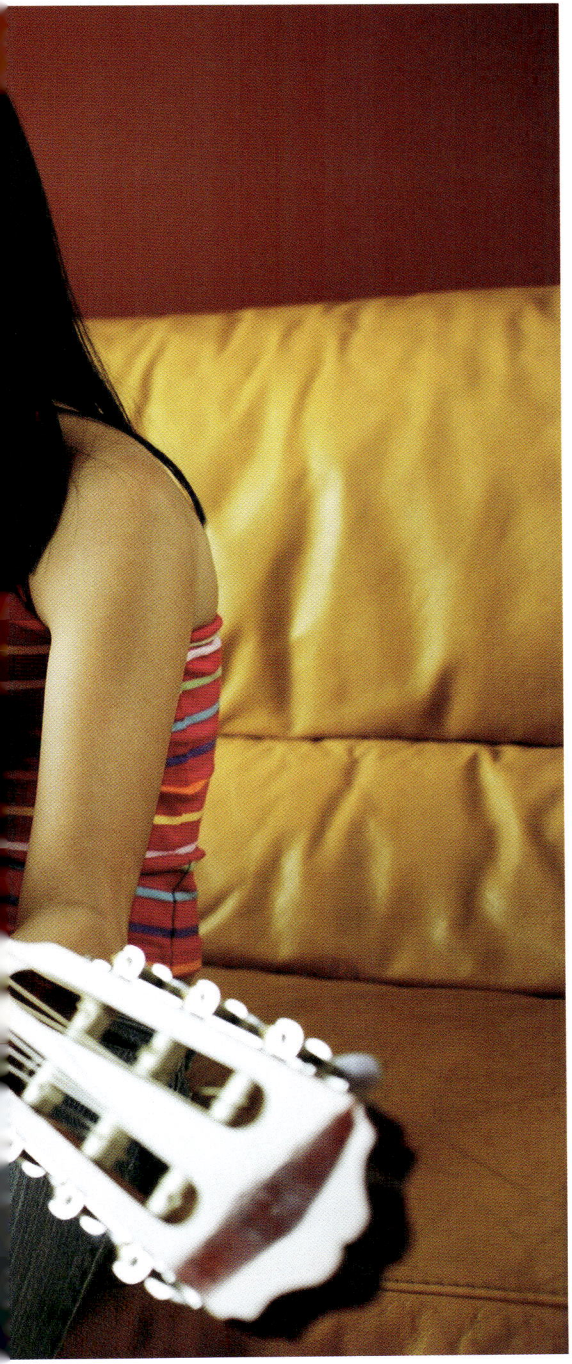

is a great **supporter**. This person could be a teacher, parent, friend, or extended family member. Supportive people help us to achieve goals by reminding us of our good **qualities**, helping us feel better if we get **discouraged**, and cheering us on along the way to our goal!

Look!

Who is someone you know who achieved a goal that you also want to achieve? What did they do to achieve their goal? What can you learn from them to help you achieve your goal?

EXTEND YOUR LEARNING

We learned a lot about goals in this book. Write down one short-term goal and one long-term goal that you would like to achieve.

Break each goal into steps. What small things can you do in order to get closer to your goal?

Get inspired! Close your eyes and imagine yourself accomplishing your goal. How do you feel?

Tell yourself something encouraging to help you take a step toward your goal. For example, "I can try my best!" or "I know if I get stuck or **frustrated**, I can ask for help!"

GLOSSARY

accomplishments (uh-KAHM-plish-muhnts) things people work toward and achieve

audition (aw-DIH-shuhn) to try out for something

discouraged (dih-SKUHR-ijd) feeling disheartened or unconfident

experience (ik-SPEER-ee-uhns) prior knowledge

frustrated (FRUH-stray-tuhd) disappointed or upset

mentor (MEN-tor) a person who guides or encourages another person

pilot (PYE-luht) someone who is trained to fly a plane

progress (PRAH-gruhss) movement toward a goal

qualities (KWAH-luh-teez) characteristics or features

role model (ROHL MAH-duhl) a person who sets an example for others

strive (STRYV) to try hard

supporter (suh-POHR-tuhr) someone who encourages or helps another person

FIND OUT MORE

Books

Clinton, Chelsea. *She Persisted: 13 American Women Who Changed the World.* New York, NY: Philomel Books, 2017.

Jordan, Deloris, and Roslyn Jordan. *Salt in His Shoes: Michael Jordan in Pursuit of a Dream.* New York, NY: Simon & Schuster Books for Young Readers, 2000.

Websites

YouTube—How to Set Goals (4 Easy Steps)

https://www.youtube.com/watch?v=a4jnPQD7pO8
Check out this video and learn four easy steps to help you achieve your goals.

YouTube—Setting SMART Goals

https://www.youtube.com/watch?v=lyl_v-O_Cds
Watch this video to learn how to break your own SMART goals down into helpful steps.

INDEX

ABOUT THE AUTHOR

Emily Rose is a school psychologist, yoga teacher, and writer for her mental wellness blog, MissMagnoliaSays.com. She enjoys helping kids and adults understand and manage their emotions and live beautiful lives. Emily lives in Dearborn, Michigan.